Science at the Edge

Artificial Intelligence

Ian Graham

Heinemann
LIBRARY

www.heinemann.co.uk/library
Visit our website to find out more information about **Heinemann Library** books.

To order:
☏ Phone 44 (0) 1865 888066
🖹 Send a fax to 44 (0) 1865 314091
💻 Visit the Heinemann Bookshop at www.heinemann.co.uk/library to browse our catalogue and order online.

First published in Great Britain by Heinemann Library, Halley Court, Jordan Hill, Oxford OX2 8EJ, a division of Reed Educational and Professional Publishing Ltd. Heinemann is a registered trademark of Reed Educational and Professional Publishing Ltd.

OXFORD MELBOURNE AUCKLAND JOHANNESBURG BLANTYRE
GABORONE IBADAN PORTSMOUTH NH (USA) CHICAGO

Designed by Tinstar Design (www.tinstar.co.uk)
Illustrations by Art Construction
Originated by Ambassador Litho Ltd.
Printed and bound by South China Printing Company Ltd. in Hong Kong/China

ISBN 0 431 14894 5
06 05 04 03 02
10 9 8 7 6 5 4 3 2 1

British Library Cataloguing in Publication Data
Graham, Ian, 1953 –
          Artificial intelligence. – (Science at the edge)
          1. Artificial intelligence – Juvenile literature
          I. Title
          006.3

Acknowledgements
The Publishers would like to thank the following for permission to reproduce photographs:
CERN p44; David Cope p37; cycorp.com p27; eurofighter.org p31; Kobal Collection/Warner Bros/ Dreamworks p53; Sandro Mussa-Ivaldi p23; NASA pp13, 24, 25, 39; Popperfoto p50; Popperfoto/ Reuters p28; principia.cybernetica.com p45; Rex Features p16; Rex Features/SIPA Press p5; Robert Harding Picture Library p20; Science Photo Library pp4, 6, 7, 8, 10, 11, 14, 15, 17, 18, 19, 21, 22, 27, 30, 32, 35, 41, 42, 43, 47, 54, 57; Science and Society p12; c1998 University of Southern California Information Sciences Institute p51

Cover photograph reproduced with permission of Science Photo Library.

Our thanks to John Kingston for his assistance in the preparation of this book.

Every effort has been made to contact copyright holders of any material reproduced in this book. Any omissions will be rectified in subsequent printings if notice is given to the Publishers.

Disclaimer
All the Internet addresses (URLs) given in this book were valid at the time of going to press. However, due to the dynamic nature of the Internet, some addresses may have changed, or sites may have changed or ceased to exist since publication. While the author and Publishers regret any inconvenience this may cause readers, no responsibility for any such changes can be accepted by either the author or the Publishers.

538

Contents

Robots to the rescue   4

Robotics, AI and a-life   6

Robots   8

Human machines   18

Intelligent machines   26

Expert systems   36

The World Wide Web as
an artificial intelligence   44

The world of a-life   46

The ethics of AI   52

Conclusion   56

Timeline   58

Glossary   60

Sources of information   63

Index   64

Any words appearing in the text in bold, **like this**, are explained in the Glossary.

Robots to the rescue

In the aftermath of an earthquake, a **robot** snake slithers through the remains of a collapsed building. It is looking for survivors. It is equipped with special **sensors** to detect body heat and a video camera to send pictures to rescuers outside the rubble.

A team of small robots swarm over a building that is in danger of collapsing. They communicate with each other and decide between themselves which of them will search different parts of the building. Meanwhile, robot fish swim around in a nearby reservoir, checking for signs of contamination of the water supply. Only a close inspection reveals that they are not real. They swim with the same motion as real fish. No one controls them. They decide where they go and how they get from place to place. If their sensors detect any chemicals that should not be there, they come to the surface and radio an alarm signal to a control centre.

In the air, robot planes circle overhead. Their video cameras send views of the ground to the disaster relief planners. Their pictures are used to map the areas that have been worst hit by the earthquake and to spot any people who need help. At a nearby chemical complex, robots crawl over storage tanks checking that there are no gas leaks.

A robot sentry stands guard in a US prison. The robot is equipped with video cameras and a radar system that gives it 360-degree vision. If anything moves, it sounds an alarm and goes to investigate.

Fact or fiction?

It sounds like science fiction, but these robots are not the product of a moviemaker's mind. They have already been built. Robots that are used as guards have been developed in the United States for civilian security work. One of these, called CyberGuard, has been in service since 1991. Robot fish swim in tanks at the Massachusetts Institute of Technology, USA and at Mitsubishi Heavy Industries in Japan. Also in Japan, robots have been developed for finding gas leaks in storage tanks and for monitoring radiation levels inside nuclear reactors. US military forces use robot planes to spy on enemy troops and robot vehicles to help with mine clearance. During the Gulf War in Kuwait in 1991, a group of Iraqi soldiers tried to surrender to a robot plane circling above them. It is thought to be the first time that a robot has taken prisoners!

This robot has been developed to identify and pinpoint risks in a high explosives storage area in the United States.

Robot guards

In Thailand, an armed robot guard has been developed for security work. Roboguard can be controlled and its weapon fired from a computer anywhere in the world via the **Internet**. A video camera shows the person controlling it what the gun is pointing at. Alternatively, Roboguard can act independently. When Roboguard is controlling itself, it uses **infrared** sensors to track people's movements and aim the gun at them. At the moment, it is mounted on a platform that can rotate to point the weapon in any direction. In future, it may be given legs so that it can walk.

Robotics, AI and a-life

Scientists working in robotics make machines that behave like human beings or animals. Researchers in artificial intelligence (AI) are developing electronic brains for **robots** so that they can think for themselves. It is a field of study that brings machines and life together. Some scientists study artificial machines and systems that behave like living creatures. But what exactly are robotics, artificial intelligence and artificial life?

Robotics

Robotics is a branch of science and technology that deals with the design and construction of robots. A robot is a machine that can carry out tasks normally done by living creatures, including people. When we hear the word 'robot', many of us think of the walking, talking mechanical people that often appear in science fiction films. But a robot need not look like a human being. It might look like an animal, or it could be a mechanical arm or a vehicle with wheels. It could be any shape or size.

Inventing robots

The word 'robot' was used for the first time in 1921 by the Czech playwright Karel Capek (1890–1938) in his play *R.U.R.* (*Rossum's Universal Robots*). It comes from the Czech word *robota*, meaning work. His play showed how robots could be good for society, but also the problems they might cause, such as unemployment among humans. The word 'robotics' was used for the first time in 1942 in a short story called 'Runaround', written by the science fiction author Isaac Asimov (1920–92).

Artificial intelligence

Many of the machines that are called robots are not intelligent. For example, the robots that build cars follow a pre-programmed set of instructions that controls their movements. They can only do the job they have been programmed to do. Other robots may be controlled by a human operator. For example, the type of robot sent to look at a suspicious car that might contain a bomb is steered and operated by a person. An intelligent robot is different. It decides for itself what to do next. To do this, it needs its own form of machine intelligence – artificial intelligence (AI). Artificial intelligence is created by using computer **programs** that copy the way the human brain works.

A-life

Artificial life, or 'a-life', is a branch of science concerned with making computer-generated creatures that behave like living creatures. These computer-creatures are created by writing computer programs. They are often very simple. Even so, the way they behave, especially in groups, can help scientists to understand why flocks or herds of real creatures behave the way they do. They can even be used to understand how large crowds of people behave. They can show how whole populations of animals grow, spread and sometimes die out. Lessons learned from a-life studies are also used to improve the way, for example, trucks make deliveries. A driver can take different routes to visit lots of customers in different places. A-life studies of how **simulated** creatures move around from place to place can help to find the best route that wastes the least time and fuel.

Computer-generated a-life fish 'swim' across the screens at the Computer Museum in Boston, USA.

Robots

The first commercial product to be called a **robot** was a mechanical arm called 'Unimate'. It was produced in the United States in the 1950s by a company called Unimation, founded by Dr Joseph F. Engelberger. Unimation stood for 'universal automation'. Engelberger was inspired to create the world's first robot manufacturing company by the science fiction stories about robots written by Isaac Asimov (see page 6). The car manufacturer General Motors installed the first Unimates. They were used to take hot metal castings out of a die-casting machine, something that was difficult for people to do safely.

Dr Joseph F. Engelberger, known as the 'Father of Robotics', developed Unimate, the first industrial robot. Unimates were installed at General Motors in 1959 and started to be used there in 1961.

Transport robots

In almost every organization, there is a need to move materials around. This is usually done using trolleys pushed by people, but intelligent machines that know where they are and where they are going can often do the job better. They can carry more weight more safely and keep track of where everything is. Some hospitals use transport robots to carry medicines and patient records to where they are needed. Factories sometimes use transport robots to keep production lines supplied with goods or to carry finished parts away. Warehouses often use intelligent storage systems that store goods in the most efficient and safe way, and find them again in a fraction of the time it would take people. Office complexes sometimes use robots to transport documents and mail.

There is no reason for intelligent transporter robots to be confined within buildings. They could be used on the public roads and railways to transport all sorts of goods or people. Driverless trains are already used in some airports, including London's Gatwick Airport and the AirTrain service at New York's JFK Airport in the United States. So far, driverless vehicles have not been allowed to travel on public roads. But as the electronic 'brains' that control robot vehicles improve, we may indeed see such vehicles on our roads. Many people worry about the safety of driverless vehicles. However, the majority of accidents are caused when drivers make mistakes, so intelligent driverless vehicles could actually improve safety on road and rail.

Robots – good or bad?

Every new technology has advantages and disadvantages. Robots are no different. One advantage they have is that they can free people from the need to do dirty, dangerous or boring jobs. They can move products around a factory, work in the deadly radioactive parts of a nuclear power station and explore deep underwater. They can improve the quality of the work done. And, because robots have to be designed, built, sold, installed, operated, supervised, repaired and maintained, they also create jobs. However, they are used for tasks that would have been done by people, and can do those tasks hour after hour without a break or a holiday. This means that robots replace many of the workers who would normally have done those jobs.

Helping hands

When a motorist has an accident on a major road, the emergency services usually arrive quite quickly. However, research has shown that if help could reach accident victims just five minutes sooner, even more lives could be saved. One answer, being developed at the University of California at San Diego, USA, is a robot emergency vehicle. An intelligent computer system monitors the roads and recognizes when people are in trouble. It alerts the emergency services and sends out the robot, called Robotar. Robotar leaves its roadside 'hutch' and drives along the side of the road towards the accident. Its on-board intelligence enables it to steer around anything that gets in its way.

When Robotar reaches the scene, its cameras show the emergency services close-up pictures of the accident. Its communications system lets them talk to the people involved in the accident while they wait for help. The pictures help the emergency services to tell how severe the accident is. It also helps them to get the right people and equipment to the scene quickly.

HelpMate robots are used to transport food, papers and medical supplies in hospitals.

Service robots

When accident victims get to hospital, they may find more robots at work there. In 1988 Danbury Hospital in Connecticut, USA, was the first hospital to use a robot, called 'HelpMate'. HelpMate carries up to 100kg of medicine, food or patients' records around hospitals. It uses **sonar** and heat **sensors** together with navigation **software** to find its way around a building without bumping into things. It can ask people to move out of its way and even operate lifts on its own. In Germany, the Fraunhofer Institute has developed a robot called Care-O-Bot to help elderly and frail people stay independent. Japanese industry and academic experts predict that in less than fifteen years, intelligent personal robots will be as common as home computers are now.

Robo-medicine

Robots have already been used in hospitals to do more than carry medicines. Surgical robots have operated on brains, hearts and hip joints. One robot surgeon, called Robodoc, has taken part in more than 8000 hip replacement operations. It can drill a hole in a leg bone more accurately than a human surgeon. This means that the artificial joint that goes inside the hole fits better. A tighter fit means that the joint is less likely to work loose.

A medical robot called Pathfinder is designed to take samples of tumours (growths) or implant electrodes at very precise locations in patients' brains. Normally, this is done by screwing a metal cage to the patient's skull to guide a surgeon's instrument. Using Pathfinder, a surgeon programs the robot with the best path through the brain for the instrument. The robot then moves the instrument through the brain to precisely the right spot.

Another medical robot under development in France is so small that it can be swallowed. As it moves along inside the patient, a tiny revolving wheel measures the length of the gut. On the way, it can sample the contents. When it reaches the right spot, it can use a scalpel or another tool to perform surgery, or it can release a dose of drugs. An even smaller robot works inside blood vessels. In 1999, scientists in Germany created a robot as thin as a matchstick. Its three segments move along by pushing or pulling, one by one, like an earthworm.

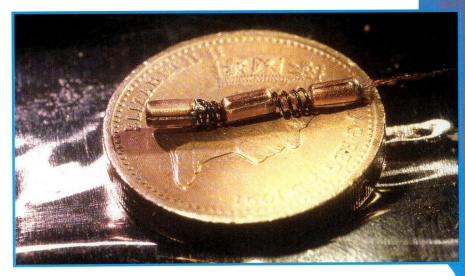

One of the smallest medical robots built so far is designed to thread its way through blood vessels like an earthworm.

Blood-bot

One of the most common ways of investigating a patient's problems is to test a blood sample. The sample is taken by pushing a hollow hypodermic needle into a vein in the arm and drawing blood out through it. Some health professionals are better than others at taking blood samples. Sometimes, they find it difficult to locate a suitable vein or to insert the needle to precisely the right depth. If they get it wrong, the patient can suffer painful bruising.

Now, scientists at Imperial College in London have developed a robot that can take blood more reliably than a person. The robot finds the vein by prodding the patient's arm and measuring how much the skin pushes back. The size of this force tells the robot whether muscle, fat or a blood vessel lies underneath the skin. It can locate a vein in this way to within one millimetre. So far, a human operator has supervised the machine and given the final go-ahead. As the needle goes in, the size of the force pushing back on it tells the robot exactly when it enters the vein.

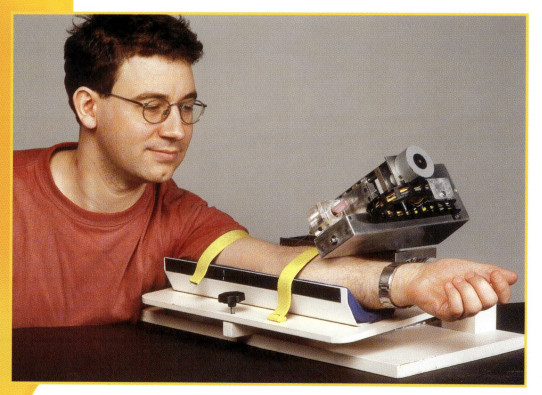

Alex Zivanovic looks on as his invention, a robot designed to take blood samples, probes his arm.

The spider-like Skyworker robot is designed to help astronauts build and repair space stations and other large structures in orbit.

Extra-terrestrial explorers

Robots can help people in outer space, too. We have been sending machines into space since 1957. These early unmanned spacecraft were either automatic machines or they were controlled directly from Earth. When an unmanned spacecraft lands on a distant planet or moon, however, a radio signal takes so long to reach it that the craft cannot be controlled by someone on Earth. Vehicles built to explore distant planets and their moons will therefore need to be intelligent enough to make their own decisions about where to go and what to do. One **prototype** space explorer robot, called Hyperion, is designed to make its own way across the surface of a distant world. It knows where it is, because it monitors the position of the Sun.

Construction workers in space

The astronauts who live in large space structures may not be able to do all the work needed to build and maintain them. Space robots are being built to help. The US space agency, **NASA**, has built Robonaut. This is a robot with a head, body, arms and hands. With hands, it can use the same tools that human astronauts use. However, Robonaut is not intelligent. An astronaut controls it. Special glasses show the astronaut the view from the cameras in Robonaut's head. Special gloves worn by the astronaut make Robonaut's hands move when the astronaut's hands move. Sensing things and moving things at a distance like this is called telepresence. Another space robot, called Skyworker, is being designed to help astronauts. It can carry loads 1000 times heavier than itself. The value of space robots is that they will reduce the risks to astronauts by reducing the number of **space walks** they will have to make. When astronauts begin to explore the planets, robots will probably go ahead of them to prepare the way. NASA may send robots to Mars to build a camp on the planet's surface before the first astronauts arrive.

Unmanned vehicles

Unmanned vehicles have been used for decades. In the past, a driver some distance away, sending control signals along a cable or by radio, controlled them. These remotely controlled vehicles, or ROVs, are still used, but now intelligent vehicles are taking to the air, land and water. They can carry out missions on their own without any human control. These vehicles are described as **autonomous**. Examples of unmanned vehicles include the Docklands Light Railway in London and the Sydney Harbour Link in Australia. Urban Robot, or Urbie, is a small military robot designed to carry out reconnaissance (spy) missions in towns. Urbie's operator simply has to click a pointer on a screen to indicate objects that Urbie can see using its video cameras. The robot then finds its own way to them. It automatically avoids obstacles without having to be steered by anyone.

Robot divers

Manned and remotely operated vehicles are used to carry out exploration and research under the sea. Most of them need constant human control during dives that last for a few hours. Now, thanks to developments in artificial intelligence, autonomous underwater vehicles (AUVs) carry out missions without human control. Some of them can stay underwater for up to a year. One AUV, the Autonomous Benthic Explorer (ABE), has carried out seabed surveys of natural features such as underwater lava flows. Another AUV, Odyssey II, has carried out dives to a depth of 1400 metres.

The Raptor unmanned plane first flew in 1993. It can navigate itself during flights which can last longer than 48 hours.

Air and space

In the air, unmanned aerial vehicles (UAVs) are already used by military forces for spy missions. Most of them are piloted by an operator on the ground. But a new generation of UAVs are designed to fly missions on their own. One of them, Global Hawk, is a jet-plane that can fly non-stop for up to 36 hours at heights of up to 20,000 metres. In 2001, it flew itself 13,000 km (8078 miles) from the United States to Australia without any human intervention.

NASA has tested autonomous systems, called remote agents, to control its **space probes**. One such probe, called Deep Space 1, was launched in 1998 and carried a remote agent capable of planning and carrying out activities on board the spacecraft without any help from ground controllers.

Aping nature

Some robots mimic living creatures. Six-legged robots copy the walking action of insects. Others copy the wavelike motion of snakes, fish and worms. Building robots that copy real creatures is called biomimetics.

The first robo-fish (pictured below) was a copy of a tuna fish built in 1994 at Massachusetts Institute of Technology, USA. Robo-fish built by Japanese scientists are so realistic that only close inspection reveals that they are actually robots. Robot copies of extinct fish have been made, based on their fossils, to study how they might have moved when they swam. Results from robot fish research will also help to develop new autonomous underwater vehicles (AUVs) that can travel further and faster on the same battery power.

Mutating, or morphing, robots go one stage further. These are 'intelligent' creatures made from a series of identical segments. These creatures can join their own segments together in different ways, according to the type of ground they have to travel over. A prototype built in the USA forms itself into a wheel for rolling over flat ground, then into a spider shape for picking its way over rough ground. If it comes to a narrow gap, it can become a long thin snake to squeeze through that gap.

Robots with appetites

Most robots are powered by electricity from batteries, but this poses problems. The batteries eventually run flat. One answer is to use **solar panels** to recharge the batteries, but these take up a lot of space. Another answer is to make the robot go to an electricity socket to recharge its batteries. This might be a solution for robots that work inside buildings. Nuclear power packs, which are used to supply electricity to some spacecraft, would work well. However, the possibility of radiation leaks, and the problem of disposing of the packs safely, make them unacceptable. **Fuel cells**, which make electricity from the chemical reaction between hydrogen and oxygen, are too big and heavy at the moment and their hydrogen fuel is difficult to handle, because it is stored at very low temperatures, and under high pressure.

So, some designers are building robots that get their energy in the same way that we do – by eating and digesting food. The first 'gastrobot' was developed in 2000 at the University of South Florida, Tampa, USA. It 'eats' sugar, which is digested by bacteria and turned into electricity. This prototype is fed sugar lumps by hand, but the aim is to build gastrobots that live on natural vegetation outdoors. A lawn-mowing gastrobot could 'eat' the grass clippings it produces. Meat contains more energy than vegetation, but meat-eating robots are more difficult to develop, because natural sources of meat tend to run away! And one can't help wondering if meat-eating robots might treat people as food!

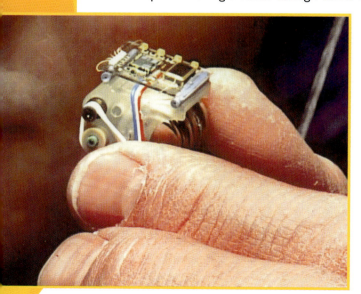

Tiny, tank-like microbots built at the US Sandia National Laboratories have a top speed of 50 cm a minute.

Small is beautiful

Robots are getting smaller. Tiny vehicles built at the Sandia National Laboratories in the USA are less than 10 mm wide. The Ant project at Massachusetts's Institute of Technology's Artificial Lab, USA, is a community of **microbots**, each of which is about half the length of a matchstick. Microbots are not the smallest robots of all. **Nanobots** are even smaller.

Scientists have built a robot arm which is just over half a millimetre long – about as long and narrow as a hyphen in this book. It was made from a **silicon** frame covered with layers of gold and plastic. It had an elbow, wrist and hand with fingers. The joints could bend. It was used to grab and move a glass bead only a tenth of a millimetre across. Equally tiny motors, propellers and even a helicopter have been made.

Scientists at the US Cornell Nanobiotechnology Center, USA, have found a way of powering tiny motors the size of **viruses**. They use the same chemical that powers living cells – a substance called adenosine triphosphate (ATP). Chemical reactions in the ATP release energy that turns the motors and propellers. So far, these tiny robots have no intelligence. However, researchers believe they might be used in future to look for particular cells inside the body and move them or kill them. They could open blocked blood vessels or kill cancer cells.

'The challenge is to devise nanomotors whose motion can be controlled externally (so that they can be used to move things around at will) and that can be refuelled.'
Flemming Besenbacher, University of Aarhus, Denmark, and Jens Noskov, Technical University of Denmark

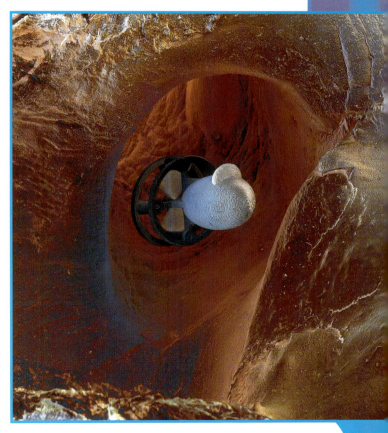

A nano-submarine sails through an artery (blood vessel), driven along by a tiny spinning propellor.

Human machines

Robot designers would like to build walking robots, because they would be able to cross rough ground and climb stairs better than robots with wheels. But it has proved to be impossible, so far, to build a machine that can walk as well as a person. A few robots can walk, but they cannot keep their balance as well as humans.

We start walking by leaning forwards. Putting out a foot in front stops us from falling over. To keep going, we keep leaning forwards and putting out each foot in turn. Each step is timed and positioned with great precision. We do it without thinking. Robots use an enormous amount of **computing power** to do the same thing, but badly. Now, instead of programming a robot with a set of instructions for walking, researchers are building machines that learn to walk in the same way as we do – by trial and error.

Dr Toshio Fukudu experiments with Brachiator 3, better known as Robo-monkey, at Nagoya University, Japan.

Monkey business

Japanese researchers are studying robot movement, not by building a walking robot, but by building a robot that hangs from an overhead ladder. 'Robo-monkey' tries to swing from rung to rung like a gibbon swinging through the trees. It has to learn how to move for itself. Video cameras can see its arms and track their movements. Every time it makes a mistake, it has to work out for itself what went wrong and try again. Robo-monkey's designers do not believe that future robots will swing through the trees, but a swinging robot does not keep falling over and does not have to balance itself, so it learns faster. Therefore, lessons learned from Robo-monkey will help with the design of walking robots.

Intelligent body parts

Research into replacement parts (called **prosthetics**) for people has benefited the development of robot limbs. Some of the latest prosthetic limbs have joints that become stiffer or more flexible according to what they have to do. They respond to the changing loads and forces they have to cope with, like real limbs and joints. Some of them are electrically powered. They are controlled by the electrical activity of nearby muscles. Robotics researchers are using these developments to help with their work on robot limbs.

Myoelectronics

In the 1770s, scientists discovered that electricity makes muscles move. The electricity that makes muscles work is not enough to power electric motors. However, it can be amplified (made bigger). If someone has lost a hand, an electrically powered artificial hand can be fitted in its place. This artificial hand takes electricity from muscles in the arm, amplifies it and uses it to power the motors that make the hand grip. An artificial arm can be powered by electricity from the shoulder muscles. Using the body's own muscle electricity to operate devices is called myoelectronics.

Robot designers are making use of the technology for creating replacement body parts to develop robot hands and limbs.

Androids

Androids are the walking, talking robots that look like human beings and are often seen in science fiction movies. They are independent, self-propelled, intelligent machines with artificial senses. We are nowhere near building a real android, but researchers, mainly in the United States and Japan, are working towards it.

When businesses started to use computers in the 1950s, people were amazed by what they could do. There were predictions that they would be the brains of advanced androids within twenty years. In fact, progress has been much slower than anyone expected. Engineers can build mechanical bodies for androids. However, developing the robot's brain has proved to be far more difficult.

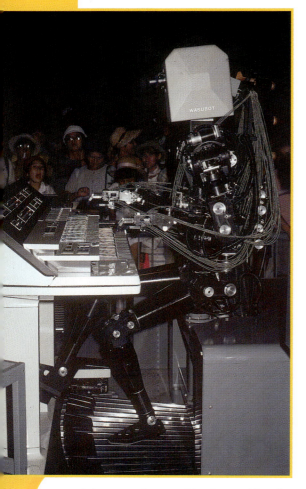

A Japanese humanoid robot tinkles the ivories. It uses artificial intelligence to find its way around the keyboard.

Androids at work

If scientists ever manage to build androids, there are lots of jobs waiting for them to do! In Japan, simple robots are already replacing men who stand in the road and wave flags to direct motorists away from road works. These robots save lives – one is hit by a car every month or so. A robot for laying traffic cones on roads is being developed in Britain. More advanced androids could take over other dangerous jobs that are currently done by people. Androids will learn in the same way as humans do. Cog, a robot developed at the Massachusetts Institute of Technology in the United States, already has vision. Now hands, touch, hearing and speech are being developed for it. Unlike a computer, Cog is not programmed to do things. It learns how to do something by watching a person doing it and copying. It uses trial and error. If it makes a mistake, it tries something different next time.

Android senses

We have five senses – sight, smell, taste, touch and hearing. An android need not have precisely the same five senses. Sight and hearing are obviously important if an android is to see where it is going and respond to sounds, including speech. Touch is important, too, so that an android knows when it has bumped into something, or so it can sense how tightly its hands are holding something. Taste is unnecessary for a machine that does not eat or drink. Smell is not vital either. An android could have extra senses that we do not have. For example, it might have the ability to sense **infrared** (heat) rays. It could tell how hot something was just by looking at it.

In very simple terms, Cog is thinking. This sounds very advanced, but in fact, Cog is not as mentally capable as a two-year-old child.

Some scientists wonder if there is any point in spending huge amounts of money striving to develop walking, talking androids. In the end, it may prove to be impossible. Even if it is possible, it may turn out to be a waste of effort. Simpler machines can be designed to do just one or two particular jobs better than a general-purpose android could do them. Other scientists disagree. They think that all the cost and effort is justified, because robots that look like us, and walk and talk like us, will be more acceptable to our society.

'We have an image of robots as partners, and a machine similar to humans can evoke shared feelings.'
Masato Hirose, designer, Honda Motor Corporation

The US robot, Cog, tries out its new fingers. Cog learns by watching people through its cameras and then copying them.

Cyborgs

While androids are human-looking robots, cyborgs are part human, part machine. The human body is weak. Our memory is often faulty, and our senses sometimes fail us. There are machines and computers that have better memories and senses. One line of robotics research aims to improve the human body and brain by replacing parts of them with artificial parts that may work more efficiently. In fact, this already happens to a certain extent. Cochlear implants restore hearing to the deaf, prosthetic limbs replace missing limbs and light-sensitive devices have been implanted experimentally inside the eyes of a few blind people to study the possibility of restoring sight.

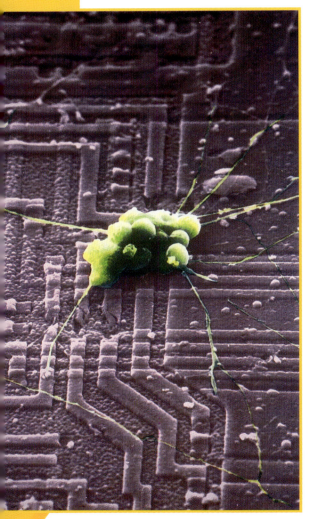

The research is a long way from being able to dramatically alter human beings. Its humble beginnings involve hooking up individual living cells with **silicon** chips in the laboratory. In 1995, scientists at the Max Planck Institute of Biochemistry in Munich, Germany, connected a nerve cell from a rat to a silicon chip. Researchers at Stanford University, USA, have succeeded in joining living nerves to silicon chips and passing electrical impulses between the two.

Brain control

Part of the brain of a lamprey, a type of fish, has been used to control the movements of a small-wheeled vehicle. This part of the brain normally keeps the lamprey upright in the water. In the robot, it is connected up to control electric motors that turn the robot's wheels. In this way, the fish brain steers the robot. In another experiment, scientists wired a water feeder into a rat's brain.

A human nerve cell grows across a silicon chip. Scientists have succeeded in wiring nerves and chips together.

The rat, which used to operate the feeder by pushing a lever, learned to operate it simply by thinking about it. This often controversial research aims to help develop artificial limbs that are wired directly into the brains of their owners. The new limbs are moved by their owners simply willing them to move, just like a real limb.

In 1996, surgeons at the Radcliffe Infirmary in Oxford, England, succeeded in connecting a patient's brain directly to a computer. The patient had been paralyzed from the neck down in a road accident. Electrodes implanted in his brain were wired into the computer, enabling him to move a cursor (pointer) on the computer's screen. The system improved the patient's ability to communicate with other people.

Professor Sandro Mussa-Ivaldi is shown here holding the lamprey fish brain he used to steer a robot towards a light source.

Robots with wet brains

Biological brains are also called 'wetware' to distinguish them from silicon chips (hardware) and computer programs (software). There are distinct advantages in using wetware instead of silicon chips to control a robot. Most computers need precise, correct and complete information or they will not come up with the correct answer. But wetware is very good at making sense of the sort of incomplete or inaccurate information we often have to cope with in the real world. At the Georgia Institute of Technology, USA, scientists made a wetware computer from nerve cells taken from a leech. They then taught this computer to do simple sums. The leech computer is little more than a simple calculator, but the ultimate aim of this research is to produce a living brain for a robot.

'This is trespassing on nature but scientists do that all the time. It's worth it if it leads to new knowledge and better prosthetic limbs.'
Professor Sandro Mussa-Ivaldi of Northwestern University, Evanston, Illinois, USA, who developed the lamprey-controlled robot

Robot muscles

So far, most robots have moved their limbs, hands and fingers by using electric motors to pull wires connected to the body parts. However, these are bulky and complicated, so are difficult to design, expensive to make and have lots of moving parts to break. A new type of robot 'muscle' replaces all the motors and wires with a plastic material called electroactive polymer (EAP). EAP muscles work by changing shape when electricity is applied to them. Bundles of EAP fibres lengthen or shorten like real muscle fibres without any need for motors, gears or control wires. They also need a fraction of the electricity that motorized body parts need. This makes EAP-powered body parts simpler, lighter and less likely to break down. These factors, together with their low power consumption, make EAP body parts very attractive to spacecraft designers. A **prototype** palm-sized robot vehicle designed to land on an asteroid was fitted with wipers moved by EAP muscles to keep dust off the windows in front of its instruments.

Research in one field of science or technology is often applied in a completely different field. Robotics research sometimes throws up developments that benefit humans. EAP research, which aims to provide robots with human-like muscles, may end up being applied to human medicine. Researchers are studying whether EAP muscle fibres could one day replace or assist damaged human muscles.

The NASA 'Nanover' space robot pictured above uses tiny wipers powered by EAP muscles to keep its instruments clean.

Fuzzy logic

Computers usually treat information as either one thing or another – on or off, true or false, black or white, hot or cold. However, things are rarely one extreme or the other in the real world. For example, it might be freezing cold, chilly, cool, mild, warm, hot or boiling. Robot brains need to be able to deal with this sort of 'real-world' information. One answer is **fuzzy logic**. To a fuzzy logic system, all temperatures are treated as partly hot. So, the temperature one day might be 20 per cent hot. In addition, there might be 65 per cent sunshine, 15 per cent wind and 0 per cent rain. Combining this fuzzy information can give a computer or a robot a 'feel' for the real world. Fuzzy logic programs are already built into the computers that control car engines, washing machines, video cameras, handwriting recognition systems, earthquake prediction systems, lifts and nuclear reactors.

Electroactive polymer

There are two types of EAP that are suitable for use as robot muscles. The first is a flexible ribbon made from long chains of carbon, fluorine and oxygen molecules. When an electric current flows through the ribbon, it bends like a finger. Scientists have put several of these ribbons together to make a hand-like gripper that can pick up small rocks.

The second type of EAP muscle is made from a sheet of the material rolled into a tube. Giving the tube an electric charge makes it stretch or contract, similar to real muscle fibres.

Future robots may have human-like muscles made of EAP.

Intelligent machines

Research into artificial intelligence began soon after the first electronic computers were built in the 1940s. Scientists realized that these computers could be programmed to do things that are normally done by a human brain. For example, they could play a game by processing information according to a set of rules.

Researchers tried using the same method to make systems with more general intelligence instead of systems that just did one thing. However, this involved writing rules for every possible situation that the system, or the **robot**, might have to deal with. This has proved to be very difficult. Most AI research today takes a different approach. Instead of programming normal computers with rules, it involves building computers that have a similar structure to a human brain, so that they can learn in the same way as a brain learns.

Our brains are very good at analysing and recognizing patterns, whether these are patterns of sound in speech or patterns of light, dark and colour that give us the sensation of sight. Designing artificial systems that can recognize patterns of sound and light as expertly as humans is proving to be very difficult. However, this is a vital area of AI research in the creation of intelligent robots that we can talk to and that can understand what they see and hear.

Face to face

An intelligent machine should be able to recognize whom it is talking to, so some AI researchers are concentrating on face recognition. Humans recognize faces by using part of the brain called the fusiform face area, which is very good at spotting the differences between faces. However, scientists have not yet discovered how this brain area works. Computers recognize faces in one of two ways. One method analyses the positions of the eyes, nose and mouth. It treats them as a sort of 'facial fingerprint' to identify the owner. The second method analyses the pattern made by the whole face – a much more complex 'facial fingerprint' that contains more information.

This computer system maps the user's face. It then uses the way his or her features and expressions change to animate the traditional Japanese theatre character on the screen.

The simplest **face recognition systems** can be fooled by different facial expressions, lighting or head positions. They might recognize someone with a blank expression, but fail to recognize the same person with a broad smile. To identify people correctly, they have to see the faces looking straight ahead, with the same expression, under the same lighting. The most complex systems can cope with different expressions, positions and lighting. The best can even see through deliberate disguises. These are the most useful for scanning crowds to look for criminals, who might be disguised.

Common sense

To be genuinely intelligent, a machine needs to know about the real world. For us, that involves remembering a huge number of facts. We also need to know all the rules and ideas that link these facts together. A system called Cyc (as in 'encyclopedia') has been programmed with more than a million words, names, descriptions and ideas. They enable the **program** to learn on its own and to show some common sense. Some scientists think that Cyc is beginning to show signs that it is aware of its own existence.

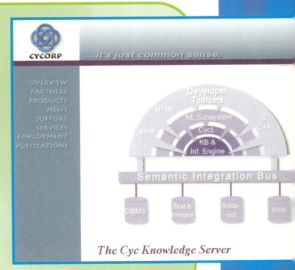

The Cyc Knowledge Server

Playing chess

Chess is a very complicated game. Different pieces move in different ways and some are more important than others. Players have to bear this in mind when working out their next move. The best players look several moves ahead, think what their opponent might do each time and then make the right move. If their opponent does something unexpected, they have to be prepared to change their game plan. Computers programmed to play chess have to copy this complex human thought process. Because of this, researchers in AI are very interested in games programs.

One of the first chess programs was written in 1948. By the 1980s, the programs were good enough to defeat experienced players. Then, in February 1996, Gary Kasparov became the first world chess champion to be defeated by a computer – IBM's Deep Blue computer.

Deep Blue was a massive machine weighing more than a tonne. The first time they met in a competition match, Deep Blue won the first game. Later, Kasparov fought back to win the match, four games to two. He was able to beat the computer by switching strategy (his game-plan) in mid-game.

Chess champion Gary Kasparov considers his next move in a match against IBM's expert chess-playing computer, Deep Blue.

The Deep Blue team spent the next year improving their player's **hardware** and **software**. In its improved form, Deep Blue could consider more than 200 million possible moves in one second. It could look six moves ahead before selecting the best move and taking its turn. Kasparov, who is one of the world's greatest chess players, could consider about three moves per second. The team also gave Deep Blue the ability to switch strategies during games. When the two met again in May 1997, Deep Blue beat Kasparov.

'It is chess that once again provides us the ability to compare man versus machine.'

Gary Kasparov, chess grand master and former world champion

Talking machines

It is not difficult to make a machine talk. Computers, electronic games and telephone answering systems all talk to us with machine voices. The first artificial voice systems passed a basic sound through filters in order to mimic the way the vocal tract (the throat, mouth, tongue and lips) changes the sound to produce words. Now, the sound is produced digitally, by computer. All information, including sound, is stored in a computer as a series of numbers. Changing the numbers changes the sound they produce.

When a machine has to speak, a computer program assembles the sounds in the correct order to make words. Up to 60 different factors shape the sound of an artificial voice. A few of them are set permanently, to give the voice its individual character. Most of them have to be varied continuously while the machine is speaking.

Robot cashiers

A talking bank cash machine called 'Stella' has been developed and publicly trialled in Canada. It recognizes individual customers by comparing the pattern in their iris (the coloured part of the eye) with the iris patterns of customers stored in its memory. It then greets customers by talking to them and asking how much money they want. The likelihood of Stella making a mistake about a customer's identity is said to be 10 billion billion to one.

The robot dog, Aibo, is one of a new generation of robot pets that can understand certain instructions that are spoken to them.

Voice recognition

Making machines understand what is said to them is much more difficult than making them talk. They have to cope with people talking at different speeds and with different accents. They also have to make sense of incorrect grammar or incomplete sentences. The first **voice recognition systems** had to be 'trained' to recognize one particular person's voice. More advanced systems can cope with any voice without training.

Simple voice recognition systems can be bought to use with home PCs. They recognize speech and convert it into text on the screen. Sony's robot pet dog, Aibo, can recognize about 50 spoken words. There are voice activated television remote controls, ovens and light switches. The systems are reliable enough today to be used in cars and aircraft. In 2000, the Jaguar S-Type car was sold with voice activated controls for the temperature, stereo system and mobile phone. The Eurofighter fighter plane is flown with the help of computers that can understand what the pilot says.

Got a question? Ask Galaxy!

The Massachusetts Institute of Technology, USA, has developed a system that can answer spoken questions on particular subjects. The system, called Galaxy, understands what is said to it and talks back. It can speak English, Spanish and Mandarin Chinese. Galaxy has been used to create telephone answering services. It downloads the information it needs from the Internet and turns it into speech. One service provides weather information. Another gives flight information and a third gives traffic information.

Building blocks

All the words we use can be broken down into a set of simple sounds, called phonemes. One type of voice recognition system looks for phonemes in speech. It then looks for groups of phonemes that go together to make up words. It is programmed with the rules of language – for example, that a sentence such as 'the dog eats the food' is made from a subject (the dog), a verb (eats) and an object (the food). Using these rules that we use to make meaningful sentences, it guesses what each sentence might be. It might come up with several different guesses. This system works badly with short sentences because there are so few clues in the words to tell the computer what the sentence is about.

Making connections

The cleverest voice recognition systems know more about the real world. They understand which words can be linked together and which combinations of words do not make sense. They know, for example, that a car's wheels turn, spin or skid, but do not walk, write or smile. They understand that rain and wetness go together, but that rain and, say, roundness do not. This means that they are more successful at making the right choice from their short-list of possible sentences. For example, a sentence might sound like 'The books were bound in leather' or 'The books were burned in leather'. This system knows that books can be either bound or burned, but 'bound in leather' makes more sense than 'burned in leather'.

If voice recognition systems become commonplace, they could change the appearance of the equipment we use every day. Our computers, televisions, radios, mobile phones, kitchen appliances and, of course, robots, will not need keyboards, knobs or switches. They will respond to voice commands. And surfing the Internet will no longer involve clicking with a mouse – you will just say what you want and your computer will find it!

A Eurofighter pilot operates some of the plane's equipment by talking to the computer that controls it, instead of pushing switches.

Intelligent conversation

In the 1968 film *2001: A Space Odyssey*, astronauts talk to their spacecraft's computer and it talks back to them as if it were a real person. In the real world of science and technology, scientists have not yet been able to build a machine that can converse intelligently on any subject as well as humans do.

Understanding what is said and then saying something back is called **natural language processing**. Perfecting it in machines has proved to be very difficult. One company has developed a program that can converse using a few words of 'baby talk'. It uses the very simple understanding of language of a 15-month-old child. They are working on a new program that will converse as well as a five year old. The program learns how to talk in the same way as a human child. It tries different answers to what is said to it and learns which are better.

Modelling emotions

One of the characteristics that makes us human is our ability to show emotion. Recognizing other people's feelings by 'reading' their body language and the expressions on their face is an important part of the way we communicate. Robot designers are trying to make their robots display feelings, or at least the appearance of feelings. Kismet is a robot

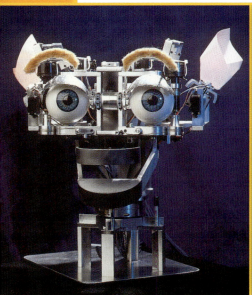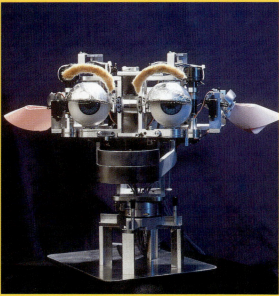

Despite its simple mechanical appearance, the US robot Kismet can show a wide range of different facial expressions, including surprise (left) and happiness (right).

designed at the Massachusetts Institute of Technology in the United States. It can show a variety of different facial expressions by moving its lips, eyelids and ears. People who 'meet' Kismet recognize these expressions and respond to them as if Kismet were human.

Robots with artificial emotions are not only found in laboratories. A toy doll called My Real Baby interacts with people and produces realistic facial expressions. However, making a robot move its mouth, eyes or ears in response to people's voices or actions is not the same as having real emotions. AI researchers are divided over the question of whether robots will experience feelings in the same way that we do. Our emotions are the result of the way we are made. Changes in the chemicals circulating through our brain and body produce physical changes. They make our heart race, or they make us sweat or shake. They make our muscles ache or they make tears well up in our eyes. Mechanical robots will never experience these chemical changes because they are made differently from humans.

'In 40 years' time, you'll be used to using conscious computers and you wouldn't buy one unless it was conscious.'

Professor Igor Aleksander, Head of Neural Systems Engineering, Imperial College, London

The Turing Test

More than 50 years ago, the British mathematician Alan Turing (1912–54) carried out pioneering work on computer science and artificial intelligence. Turing predicted that one day machines would be built that would mimic the way the human brain works. In 1950, he invented a test, now called the Turing Test, to find out whether these machines are intelligent. It works like this. One person types questions on a computer keyboard. These are received by another person and a machine, and both answer the questions. If, after some time has passed, the person asking the questions cannot tell the difference between the answers from the person and the answers from the machine, then the machine must be showing intelligence.

Teamwork

In the natural world, there are some creatures, like lions and bears, which are successful because they are big, powerful, intelligent creatures. But there are many others that are also very successful despite being small and having tiny brains with little intelligence. Their large numbers and their ability to work together more than make up for their lack of size and brainpower. Some species of ants and bees are particularly good at teamwork. They almost seem to be parts of the same communal brain.

Some robotics researchers are developing teams or swarms of small robots that can communicate with each other. This is usually done by means of invisible **infrared** beams. A beam may simply tell a robot that there is another robot working to its left, so it need not move in that direction. Or it may tell a robot what all the nearby robots are doing and what information they may have found. A swarm robot usually follows a very simple program, because of its small size. However, the swarm can achieve a great deal because of their numbers.

Building lots of small robots instead of one large robot is called **distributed robotics**. The work that has to be done is shared, or distributed, amongst a large number of robots. One advantage of distributed robotics is that a swarm of small robots can cover more ground more quickly than a single robot. This means that they can collect more information from more places. Another advantage is that it does not matter if one or two of them break down, because the rest keep going. Space scientists are particularly interested in distributed robotics. If a single robot sent to study the surface of a distant planet or moon fails, the whole costly project may be lost. But if one robot in a swarm of **microbots** fails, the rest can carry on with their work and the project can continue.

Team-bots

Some robot designers believe that creating teams of small robots is a more sensible direction for robot research than trying to build intelligent androids. The Ant project at Massachusetts's Institute of Technology's Artificial Lab, USA, is a community of microbots that work together like a colony of ants. Each fingernail-sized microbot has the same computing power as one of the first IBM desktop PCs. They communicate with each other by means of invisible infrared beams.

Teams of robot football players compete each year for the Robot World Cup. In 2001, 111 teams from more than 20 countries entered. The robots have to play without any human control. They have to

An Ant microbot stands on top of an apple. The two wires at the front tell the on-board computer when the robot hits something. Each Ant sends information to nearby microbots and receives information from them.

decide where to place themselves on the indoor field and which way to move the ball. The competition's creators predict that teams of humanoid robots will be playing for the cup within 50 years. The aim of the competition is to stimulate research into getting robots to work together. It has a serious purpose. Once teams of humanoid robots are a reality, the aim is to transform them from footballers into rescue teams. These teams could, for example, search for injured or trapped people.

'Far too many of my colleagues argue for single robots and reject the idea of colonies of nano-robots.'
Moustafa Chahine, co-founder of the Mars Pathfinder space project

Teams of robot football players from all over the world compete against each other every year for the Robot World Cup.

Expert systems

Expert systems represent one of the most successful areas of artificial intelligence. These systems are computer **programs** that mimic the knowledge and decision-making ability of a human expert on a particular subject. They can help inexperienced people to take decisions that normally have to be taken by experts. They can also act as a second opinion for experienced people. They not only improve the quality of decision-making, but they are a lot less expensive than the cost of consulting a human expert before every decision. Expert systems are used in medicine, engineering, design, business management, finance and career guidance.

An expert system has two parts. The first is the **knowledge base**. This contains thousands of facts about the subject. The second part is the inference engine. This is a set of rules that tells the system what a set of facts means. To use the system, someone types in answers to a series of questions. If the system was designed to find out why a car had broken down, the questions might be as follows: Did the engine start? Did it sound normal? Did it run down slowly or stop suddenly? Do the lights work? Is there steam or smoke coming from the engine? When it has enough information, the inference engine uses its rules to suggest what might have happened. In this example, the system works like an experienced car mechanic, matching the facts to the different faults an engine can suffer.

Rules and knowledge

The IBM Deep Blue computer that plays chess (see pages 28–29) is one example of an expert system. Deep Blue is programmed with the basic rules of chess and also the specialized chess-playing knowledge of the world's best players. Its decisions about which move to make give any chess player the ability to play like the best in the world. Medical expert systems help doctors to make the most accurate diagnoses of patients' illnesses. Financial expert systems analyse the world's financial markets and advise people whether to buy or sell stocks and shares.

Mozart lives!

In April 1997, an audience at the University of California at Santa Cruz, USA, listened to a performance of Mozart's 42nd symphony. Anyone familiar with Mozart's music would recognize it as typical of his work. However, it was written 200 years after Mozart died! Mozart wrote 41 symphonies. The 42nd was created by a computer system.

The system, called Experiments in Musical Intelligence, or EMI (pronounced Emmy), was created by composer David Cope, shown below. It does not simply take bits of Mozart's music and stick them together in a different order, because the result would not sound like Mozart's work. It is programmed with the rules of music and musical composition. It then breaks down the composer's work into short pieces in a similar way to splitting up sentences into verbs, adjectives, nouns and so on. In this way, it learns the 'grammar' and 'vocabulary' of the composer's style. This enables it to create new musical works using the same grammar and vocabulary. EMI has also produced music in the style of Bach, Beethoven, Brahms, Chopin and Scott Joplin.

Medical expert systems

Computer programs designed to diagnose diseases and other medical conditions have been available since the 1960s. These early systems were not popular. They were unreliable and they ran on huge **mainframe computers** that were slow and difficult to use. Since then the programs have improved enormously, and the cost of computer memory today is a fraction of its cost in the 1960s. So, computer systems can now store many times more information for a fraction of the cost. This means that expert systems today can call on much more knowledge than ever before. Computers have also shrunk to a fraction of their size in the 1960s, they work much faster, and are easier to use. A medical expert system today can run on a standard PC.

A doctor uses a diagnostic program by answering questions about the patient's symptoms, medical history and, perhaps, the results of tests. The system then produces a list of possible diagnoses. It may give each of them a probability. One patient's chest pains may be 80 per cent likely to be indigestion, while another patient's chest pains may be 90 per cent likely to be heart disease. The difference between them might be because of different life styles, diets and past illnesses.

We expect doctors to know what is wrong with us, but doctors are faced with more diseases and medical conditions today than ever. Fast international travel means that someone sitting in a doctor's waiting room today may have picked up a tropical bug in a foreign country just hours before. Many conditions might once have been covered by the 'catch-all' diagnosis – 'it's probably a virus'. Now, many conditions are known to be due to a variety of causes, including vitamin shortages, enzyme or hormone problems or even air pollution.

Diseases such as tuberculosis and malaria that were once thought to have been almost eradicated from developed countries are on the increase again. But doctors who have been trained in the past twenty years in these countries may not have seen them before. Expert systems help doctors by suggesting a wider variety of possible diagnoses and highlighting the most likely options. They can also reduce the cost of health care by eliminating the need for some tests, scans and even surgical procedures.

'The consumer expects the doctor to be right 90 per cent of the time, and these programs will help.'

Dr Eta S. Berner, University of Alabama, USA

Electronic noses

One of the more bizarre uses for these systems in medicine is as an artificial nose! The smell of a patient's breath can suggest conditions ranging from diabetes to liver, stomach or intestinal problems. Infected flesh often has a distinctive smell. Some doctors are better than others at detecting these smells.

However, a gas analyser equipped with artificial intelligence is better still at detecting the slightest trace of odour from breath, blood, urine, a wound or an injury and then linking it to the correct medical condition. A **prototype** 'intelligent nose' has been developed by the US Department of Energy's Pacific Northwest National Laboratory.

The JPL ENose acts like a human nose by responding with its sensors to a vast array of smells. Its reaction to the different trace vapours in the air is measured and the elements in the 'smell' are identified. Among the future uses for the ENose are environmental monitoring, food processing and medical diagnosis.

Knowledge on the Internet

The arrival of the **World Wide Web** means that the information an expert system uses need not be stored on a desktop PC. It can be stored on a large computer somewhere else, which lots of desktop PCs can communicate with through the **Internet**. One advantage of this is that the larger computer can store more information. Having all the information in one place instead of stored in lots of separate PCs also makes it easy to update.

Enormous stores of information can make an expert system slow to use. One answer is to divide it into smaller chunks, called modules. For example, each module of a medical expert system might be devoted to a particular illness or group of illnesses. One module might deal with cancer. Others might deal with heart disease, infectious diseases, joint problems and so on. When the patient's symptoms are keyed in, the system selects the modules with more detailed information about the suspected illnesses. By cutting out unnecessary information, the system works faster and is easier to use.

Emergency, or not?

When someone calls a doctor's office, the emergency services or a helpline and describes a health problem, someone has to make a judgement about how urgently that person needs help. Some people need immediate medical treatment, whilst others need to see their own doctor the same day and others can wait to make a routine appointment to see their doctor. Sorting patients according to how urgently they need treatment is called triage. There are now expert systems designed to help staff carry out triage.

A computer at the microscope

Many illnesses, especially cancers, are identified or confirmed by medical technicians who have looked at tissue samples through microscopes. Technicians often look at lots of samples a day. Some of them may only contain a few suspicious cells in a slide containing perhaps 100,000 cells, so it is easy to miss an abnormal sample. Systems designed to scan microscope slides automatically are now available. They do not replace human technicians. Instead, their machine intelligence helps to draw attention to the most suspicious cells, so that the technicians can double-check them. A system developed in New York scans one slide every five minutes. That doesn't sound very fast, but of course the system can work non-stop, day and night. As it works, it automatically stores images of the most suspicious cells for technicians to review.

Intelligent x-rays

Microscope slides are not the only samples being checked by intelligent scanning systems. The same technique is being developed to scan X-rays for abnormalities. First, the image on the X-ray is digitized – changed from a black-and-white negative picture into computer code. The code is then analysed by the system to look for patterns that are not normal. American studies using a newly developed diagnostic system to scan X-rays improved the detection of abnormalities that can cause breast cancer from roughly 80 per cent to 90 per cent or better.

DNA research

Genome research is also being aided by robot-scanning. In France the deciphering of the DNA in every human chromosome is being speeded up by the selection and cloning of specific gene colonies identified by robots and computerized systems.

'The published evidence that computers can provide doctors with powerful tools for helping in the diagnosis and treatment of disease is growing rapidly.'
Professor John Fox of the Imperial Cancer Research Fund

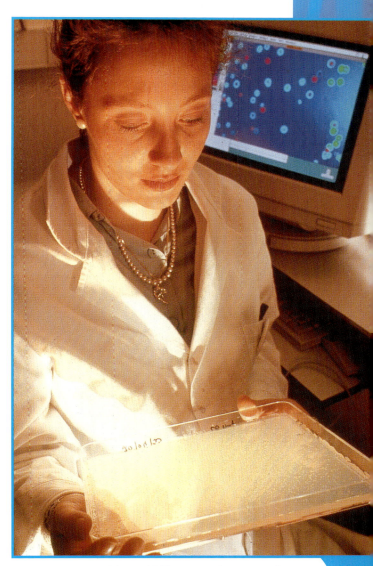

Up to 1000 gene colonies per hour can be identified and cultured by this French intelligent scanning system.

Money matters

International finance involves making **investments** through the world's stock markets. The aim is to buy stocks and shares when their prices are low and sell them again when prices rise. It sounds simple, but it is easy to get it wrong and lose money. Getting it right means being able to predict which investments are going to grow and which are not. These predictions are usually made by people with years of experience in the financial world.

As the pace of business has quickened over the years the demand for fast and accurate financial decisions has also increased. There are now expert systems programmed to study financial markets, predict their rises and falls, and suggest which investments are likely to grow. These systems work quickly and can filter and summarize vast quantities of information.

By using a financial expert system, a Swedish company increased its success rate for buying and selling shares from 60 per cent to 90 per cent. The system was developed using data from share prices over the past twenty years. It is updated every day with the latest prices. When asked for a decision on a particular investment, it applies more than 3000 rules to the data before giving its answer.

Robot profits

When IBM tested a new system for dealing in commodities (goods), they found it made more profit than people. Six computer programs called economic robotic agents, or 'bots', and six people traded against each other. The bots made 7 per cent more cash than the people. The people who developed the bots foresee a time when billions of bots will make financial decisions for businesses.

Financial institutions are experimenting with expert systems to improve their decision making.

The first businesses to use expert systems or economic bots in the financial world will make higher profits because their decision-making will be better than their competitors. However, as time goes on and more businesses use them, the differences between businesses will even out and the early gains will disappear.

Intelligent software

Ordinary computer software benefits from artificial intelligence and expert systems, too. For example, the software that finds and underlines grammatically incorrect words in Microsoft's Word word-processing program came from AI research.

A mechanical engineer designing a part for a machine often uses design software that monitors his or her activities. It anticipates what the designer wants to do and automatically brings the right features and functions up on the screen. An architect producing a drawing of a new building is automatically alerted by the software if part of the design breaks local building codes (regulations).

Design is a matter of problem solving, and problem solving is an important area of artificial intelligence. However, although machines are certainly capable of designing things, would they produce anything that we would actually want to use or wear? The design of everything from knives and forks to cars and buildings is heavily influenced by fashion, taste and culture. The curve of a car's body, the style of a dress, and the shape of a personal stereo change from year to year, mainly because of changing fashions. The clothes worn in different countries often look different, because of a country's history, traditions and culture. Artificial designers, however expert they might be, cannot incorporate these subtle factors into their designs... yet.

The programs that run computer aided design (CAD) systems are easier to use now because of their built-in intelligence.

The World Wide Web as an artificial intelligence

Artificial intelligence researchers are striving to create an artificial brain with billions of connections that make and re-make themselves like the ever-changing connections in a real brain. However, we already have an artificial system that behaves in precisely this way – the **World Wide Web**. Some people are wondering if the Web itself could be the first artificial brain.

The Web's inventor, Tim Berners-Lee, has suggested making it more intelligent by enabling it to understand the information it locates and processes. This would, for example, enable **search engines** to find more **websites** that a user really wants instead of simply listing those websites that contain key words typed in by the user.

Hardware developments are heading in the same direction. A new type of **server** (**Internet** computer), called the Principia Cybernetica Web, makes the Web work more like a brain. It was built at the Los Alamos National Laboratory in New Mexico, USA. It automatically creates new **hyperlinks** that it 'thinks' a **surfer** will want, and also disconnects old hyperlinks that are rarely used.

Tim Berners-Lee invented the World Wide Web and still heads the organization that sets Internet standards.

If this system were allowed to operate on the Internet, it would identify users as they logged on, and automatically set up the hyperlinks most useful to them on the pages they select. Different people would see different hyperlinks on the same page according to what the Internet knows about their interests. For example, a football fan might see links to football pages.

It may seem startling that the Internet could 'know' what you like. Did you know that Internet computers already track your surfing activities? They do it by using small files of data, called **cookies**. Every time you visit a website, it creates a cookie and stores it on your computer. The next time you log on to that website, it looks for the cookie to see if you have visited before and which pages you looked at. Cookies are already used to select advertisements and special offers that are best suited to a visitor's interests. In future, computer programs called agents could take this one step further. They could scan Web pages looking for items of interest to you and automatically set up hyperlinks to those pages.

> 'The global communication network is already capable of complex behaviour that defies the efforts of human experts to comprehend.'
>
> Daniel Dennett, director, Center for Cognitive Studies,
> Tufts University, Medford, Massachusetts, USA

The thinking Web

By analysing information and making decisions about it, some scientists believe the Web would be doing what we call thinking when a real brain does the same thing. In a real brain, each brain cell touches thousands of others. Together, they produce countless different pathways for nerve impulses to travel through the brain. Every time we sense something or have a thought, some of these pathways are strengthened, while others weaken. In an intelligent Web, when information is located by making new links, later searches for the same information would be quicker and easier. They would reinforce existing connections, just like a real brain using existing pathways to activate a memory. A few researchers believe that this new intelligent Web could become a 'global brain', capable of independent thought.

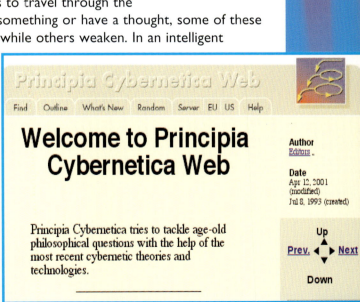

New types of Internet server, such as the Principia Cybernetica Web, aim to make the Web work more intelligently.

The world of a-life

Artificial life, or a-life, involves copying living creatures in computers. The study of artificial life began with the work of John von Neumann in the 1920s. He suggested that life-like behaviour could be produced by using a set of simple rules. The simplest example of artificial life is based on a grid of squares like a chessboard. A few of the squares contain a blob representing a creature. These blobs are called cellular automata. The rules that govern their behaviour might be as simple as:

- a blob with less than two neighbours dies
- a blob with more than three neighbours dies
- a group of exactly three blobs can spawn a new blob.

Each time the computer calculates what happens to all the creatures and plots their new positions, this represents a new generation. Sometimes, after a few generations, the whole population dies out. With a slightly different starting pattern or with slightly different rules, the population might grow.

These simple creatures may seem to have little to do with the real world. However, real creatures in a crowd or herd often move according to quite simple rules, like these. For example, each person in a crowd trying to leave a building moves forward, if there is room, towards a door. Modelling the behaviour of a crowd of people enables the designers of sports arenas to place the crowd barriers and emergency exits in the best positions to let people enter and leave safely. The same techniques have been used to create life-like crowds of computer-generated creatures in movies.

Neural networks

The human brain works differently from a **desktop** PC. A PC generally does one calculation after another until a problem is solved. A brain splits problems up into many smaller parts. It then processes the parts in different areas of the brain at the same time. At any moment, millions of brain cells are firing at the same time, processing information. Computers can be made that work this way, using a system that is called parallel processing. A computer that works more like a real brain is called a **neural network**.

Inside the brain

A human brain is made from 100 to 200 billion nerve cells called neurons. These have thousands of projections called dendrites sticking out from them, like branches on a tree. The dendrites touch up to 250,000 surrounding neurons. Together, they form a neural network with trillions of interconnections. An **artificial neural network** (ANN) mimics this system. Instead of living cells, it is made from electronic information processing units connected by wires. It can also be **simulated** by a **program** running in a normal computer. This type of network exists only in the computer's memory.

Neural networks cannot be programmed like a 'normal' computer. Instead, they are 'trained' by being given a set of data with inputs and associated outputs. They then process information over and over again through different sets of connections until they produce the best results that fit the data set. When a human or an animal does this, it is called learning.

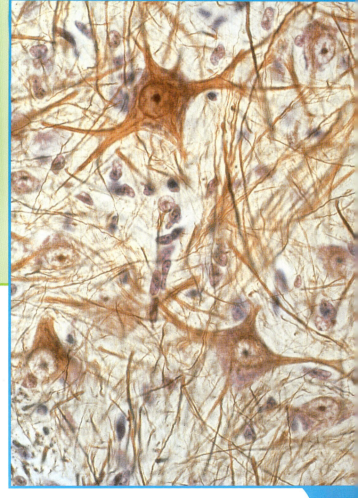

'These networks [ANN] mimic the human brain, in that they can be trained to recognize specific disease categories. Ultimately we hope that ANNs will greatly aid in the diagnosis and classification of human disease states.'
Dr Stephen J. Meltzer, Professor of Medicine at the University of Maryland, USA

Brain cells send out finger-like dendrites that touch surrounding cells and produce numerous paths for information to travel along through the brain.

Using neural networks

Artificial neural networks are cropping up in more and more places. Some **expert systems** use them to analyse data. Military forces use them to analyse information from battlefields. Game and toy designers are beginning to build neural networks into their products. In fact, the most complex artificial brain built in 1999 was not developed for artificial intelligence experiments in a research laboratory. It was developed for a toy. At a time when artificial neural networks usually contained a few hundred artificial brain cells, more than 37 million were put together to form a brain for a toy cat **robot** called Robokoneko. Its brain cells are connected together by a specially developed computer chip that allows them to form connections in the same way as real cells in a human brain.

Military applications

Military planners are investigating ways of using neural networks. Computers, video and radio equipment are now so small and lightweight that soldiers, vehicles, robots and even individual missiles can use them to relay pictures and data to a military command centre. The sheer amount of information flooding in from military operations today can make it difficult to make sense of the situation. Military forces are experimenting with the use of neural networks to analyse this information faster than conventional computers.

In the mid-1990s, the US Office of Naval Research used a neural network copy of part of a rabbit's brain to detect faults in military helicopter rotors before the rotors failed. It worked better than the mechanical systems normally used for this. Neural networks are also already used to help pilots to spot hidden targets on the ground and then aim weapons at them.

Conscious robots?

No one really understands why we are conscious and aware of ourselves, but some scientists think it may simply be due to the complexity of the human brain. Artificial neural networks are becoming bigger and more complex all the time. It is only a matter of time before scientists build neural networks that are as complex as the human brain. Some researchers think it may happen within 30 to 50 years. They wonder if these networks will become conscious and aware of their own existence purely because of their complexity. If not, then there must be another secret to our consciousness that we have not yet discovered.

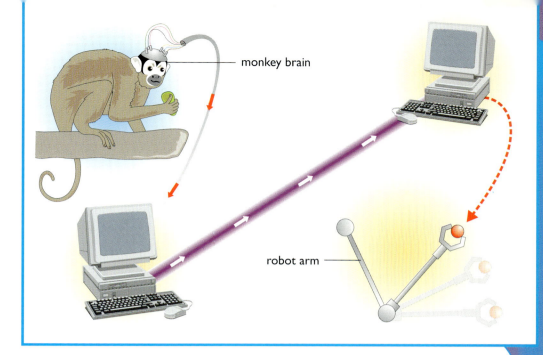

monkey brain

robot arm

Scientists have used a monkey's brain to control the movements of a robot arm 950 km (590 miles) away.

Monkey-powered robots

In the year 2000, signals from a monkey's brain were used to control a robot arm 950 km (590 miles) away. The monkey was alive and well throughout the experiment. When it reached out its arm, the electrical signals from its brain that made its arm move were fed into an artificial neural network. The network learned to change this complex electrical brain activity into the signals needed to move the robot arm in the same way. So, when the monkey reached out its arm, the robot arm reached out, too.

This line of neural network research could benefit medical research and, one day, help people who have lost limbs in accidents, by taking human brain waves and using them to control an artificial limb. Neurosurgeons predict that a system like this could also enable a severely disabled person to control the movements of his or her wheelchair by the power of thought.

'The idea of driving robotic limbs with what effectively amounts to the mere power of thought was once in the realm of science fiction. But this goal is edging closer to reality.'
Professor Sandro Mussa-Ivaldi, of Northwestern University,
Evanston, Illinois, USA

Virtual robots

In industry today, computers use **computer simulations** to test machines before they are built. Electric fans and complete airliners are just two of the products that have been tested in this way. A virtual model of the object is programmed into a computer. Its designers can then check if any parts get in each other's way, or if any become too hot or are not strong enough.

DK-96

Robots can be **simulated** inside computers, too. In 1995, a music promotion company in Japan hatched the idea of creating the world's first virtual pop star. The result was Kyoko Date, or DK-96. She looked so realistic that when photographs of her were sent to magazine publishers, some of them mistook her for a real person. Kyoko Date released her first record on 21 November 1996.

Cyber characters

Since DK-96, a French virtual pop star called Eve Solal, a British virtual pop star called T-babe and a virtual fashion model called Webbie Tookay have been created. The movements of most virtual characters have to be pre-programmed, like the actions of an **industrial robot**. A virtual newsreader called Ananova is more advanced. Her movements are animated in **real-time** as she reads news stories on the Web. Researchers are now working on virtual robot versions of **cyber** stars that can move and talk independently without a programmer or game player having to control them. However, it may be some time before such advanced virtual robots become widely available.

Japanese virtual pop star DK-96 has a lifelike face created by a team of ten computer programmers.

Adele is a virtual teacher who appears in an online service used to train medical and dental students to make diagnoses.

Robot teachers

In the United States, two **virtual robots**, called Steve and Adele, have been created at the University of Southern California Center for Advanced Research in Technology for Education. Students training as naval engineers use Steve by wearing a **virtual reality** (VR) helmet. Video screens inside the helmet let the students look into the **three-dimensional** world the robot teacher inhabits. The students can interact with the virtual teacher, too. By wearing VR gloves, students can pick up, hold and move virtual objects around in the virtual classroom. Adele (Agent for Distance Learning Environments) is an animated figure used to help train medical and dental students.

Intelligent games

Games programmers are turning to artificial intelligence to make their games more challenging. Computer games usually incorporate a set of rules that make characters on the screen behave in a certain way. Their predictable behaviour is easy for an experienced player to learn and then defeat. By giving game characters artificial intelligence, they can be made less predictable and therefore more difficult to overcome. In another development, artificial intelligence is now being used in computer games to learn how the human player behaves and to adapt the game to match that player's style and abilities.

Robot reproduction

Living creatures have the ability to reproduce and to evolve (to adapt to changing conditions over many generations). Scientists have already created computer simulations of robots that can reproduce and evolve. For example, at Brandeis University in Massachusetts, USA, a computer was set the task of designing a robot that could move itself along. The designs that were the most successful were allowed to 'evolve' into a new generation of even better designs, while less successful designs 'died out'. After 600 generations, the system was allowed to build its design. It worked. It showed that robots could design other robots.

The ethics of AI

The development and use of intelligent systems is running ahead of the laws that were created to protect us and our privacy. AI raises ethical issues that concern all of us.

Rights

Many of our cities are now monitored by closed circuit television (CCTV) systems. The pictures can be fed into intelligent **face recognition systems** that search for criminals. Many people are happy to have criminals detected by either video surveillance or intelligent face recognition, but we are less happy to be scanned ourselves. When the crowds of people who attended the 2001 Superbowl (the American football championship game) found out that they had been scanned by a face recognition system without their knowledge, many of them were outraged. **Voice recognition systems** are now being used to help answer telephone callers' enquiries. In most cases, we can tell we are talking to a machine. But in the near future, these systems will be so good that we will not know whether we are talking to a person or a machine. If we are going to be given advice by a machine, should we have the right to know that we are not talking to a person?

We accept that we have rights. Should intelligent machines have rights, too? Should they be the same as human rights? If a machine thinks like a human, is it ethical to turn it off? Do **robots** have the right to be free of pain? Pain is unpleasant, but it is important for our protection. A sharp pain can make you take your hand off a hot kettle before you get badly burned. So, perhaps it is more ethical to ensure that robots do feel pain.

Responsibilities

Rights always bring responsibilities. Our responsibility to protect future generations raises a question about robot research. Many robot researchers think it is only a matter of time before robots are more intelligent than us. At that point, we would lose our dominant position as the most intelligent species on the Earth. No one knows how this new machine species would treat humans or the planet. It could herald a new age of amazing advances in science and technology or it could threaten our own survival.

The laws of robotics

The science fiction author Isaac Asimov (1920–92) proposed three laws of robotics, which should be programmed into all robots. They are:

- Law One: A robot must not injure a human being, or, through inaction, allow a human being to come to harm.
- Law Two: A robot must obey orders given to it by human beings.
- Law Three: A robot must protect its own existence.

Later, he added a fourth law, which he called the 'zeroth' law. Law One deals with how robots should treat individual people. The new Law Zero broadens this out to include humanity (the whole of mankind):

- Law Zero: A robot may not injure humanity or, through inaction, allow humanity to come to harm.

A robot has to follow these laws, unless doing so would break a more important law. For example, if a robot is commanded to kill someone, it is allowed to refuse (breaking Law Two), because Laws Zero and One are more important.

The film *A.I.* tells the story of an android boy who has been programmed to believe he is a real boy who loves the mother who adopted him.

Robot wars

Another ethical concern is the use of military robots. Having the best technology is an important aid to winning battles. Robots and **autonomous** vehicles are already being used in military conflicts. As their numbers increase, they could begin to change the nature of warfare, just as the aeroplane, tank and submarine did.

Is it ethical to use military robots?

Up to now, the use of military robots has been limited to using them to gather information. However, future military robots could be used to actually fight. Using robots could save human soldiers from being killed or wounded. At first thought, this seems to be a good thing. However, it could make war more likely. If it were robots that were destroyed on the battlefield instead of people, a country would have less to lose from waging war. War could therefore become more common.

Navlab II is a US Army truck that is driven by a computer called Alvinn (which stands for 'Autonomous Land Vehicle in a Neural Network'). Alvinn is equipped with special collision avoidance software and is programmed to respond to road markings and junctions in the same way that a human driver would.

There is, however, another way to look at this. If one side in a war has a technological advantage through the use of robots, that side should win the war quickly. A short war should mean fewer casualties. In addition, military robots might be better than human soldiers at locating enemy troops and using weapons on them more accurately. Their use might spare more civilian lives. From this point of view, the use of military robots would be the ethical thing to do.

The question of blame

If something goes wrong, from a faulty kettle to a crashed train, we often look for someone to blame. If a robot is intelligent enough to make its own decisions, would it be the one to blame for an accident? If a driverless bus crashes, or a home help robot steps on your pet cat, who is to blame? It might be the engineers who designed and built the robot. It could be the computer programmers who taught it what to do. It could the company that sold the robot. Or, if the robot's behaviour is the result of its own learning process, could the robot itself be to blame? If intelligent robots make their own decisions, then they may be held responsible for their actions. Taking this to its logical conclusion, might we see robots standing trial in a court of law one day? That raises the interesting question of what a suitable punishment might be for a robot found guilty of a crime!

'You'll never get a computer to think until you've figured out how to get it to hallucinate.'
David Galernter, Professor of Computer Science, Yale University, USA

God's will?

The creation of conscious, intelligent machines is seen by some people as man taking on the role of a god as a creator of new forms of life. However, many religious people believe that human intelligence and free will, which made the development of robots possible, came from God. On the other hand, humans often do things that a supreme being could not possibly approve of. Perhaps, some believers argue, the creation of machine-based life is a mistake, and the creation of life, whether natural or artificial, should be left to God.

Conclusion

Progress in artificial intelligence has been slower than many researchers predicted when the work began. In the 1950s, scientists forecast that **voice recognition** would be developed and in widespread use by the 1980s. It has taken another twenty years to turn the research into working systems.

AI research can make use of the **computing power** of the biggest and most powerful computers in the world. But when AI systems are built into small independent **robots**, the amount of computing power that can be put in their small frames becomes a critical element in their design and capabilities. The amount of computing power that can be built into a given space, and its cost, have been a problem in the past. But as time goes on, both of these problems are disappearing. The amount of computing power that can be bought for US$1000 is doubling every one to two years. And the pace of computer miniaturization is such that the computing power of a **desktop** computer of a few years ago can now be squeezed into the area of a postage stamp today.

All areas of AI research and robot development are progressing increasingly rapidly now. However, the work is very different around the world. Some research teams are working on voice recognition. Others are teaching **humanoid** robots to walk. Yet others are teaching robots to understand the world around them. When all these different threads of research are pulled together in a new generation of intelligent robots, probably within in the next twenty years, we should see a sudden leap forward in the use of robots. Predictions by people working in artificial intelligence suggest that we will all be using robots and AI in the near future in much the same way as we use telephones, computers and the **Internet** today.

Predicting the effect of AI and robotics on our society and us is more difficult. AI gives companies, law enforcement agencies and governments the power to access, combine and analyse information about us faster and more powerfully than ever. This could threaten our freedom and our right to privacy. And if intelligent systems that can listen to us and talk back become commonplace in our homes, it is difficult to predict how they might alter the way we relate to others human beings.

In 1909, the author E. M. Forster wrote a story entitled 'The Machine Stops'. It describes a future world in which people live underground in homes where 'The Machine' provides all their needs for information, services, entertainment and companionship. As a result, they are incapable of functioning without it. Could this really happen to us? Will robots enhance and enrich our world and our lives as we hope? Or will they isolate us from each other and lead us into Forster's nightmare world? No one knows.

'Artificial intelligence is no match for natural stupidity.'
Anonymous

Some scientists think it may be possible within the next 50 years to build a robot brain that rivals the human brain. The implications for the human race are difficult to imagine.

Timeline

400 BC Archytas of Tarentum is reputed to have made a wooden dove that could flap its wings.

1533 In Germany, Johann Müller is said to have made a mechanical fly and eagle that could actually fly.

1645 Blaise Pascal develops his first calculating machine, which can add and subtract.

1694 Baron Von Leibniz develops a calculating machine that can also multiply.

1880 Wilhelm Roentgen experiments with applying electricity to rubber bands – research that will lead eventually to the development of electrically operated plastic muscles for **robots**.

1921 The Czech playwright Karel Capek invents the word 'robot'.

1942 The word 'robotics' is used for the first time by the science fiction author Isaac Asimov in his short story, 'Runaround', which also includes his original three laws of robotics.

1943 Warren McCulloch and Walter Pitts develop the idea of the **artificial neural network** that can learn.

1949 William Grey Walter builds a pair of machines called Elmer and Elsie that behave like robot tortoises.

1950 Alan Turing devises the Turing Test, which tests whether a computer is behaving in an intelligent way.

1954 The first modern robot, an **industrial robot** called Unimate, is developed.

1956 The term 'artificial intelligence' is used for the first time at a robotics conference at Dartmouth College, USA.

1966 The Stanford Research Institute in the USA builds Shakey, the first mobile robot that can reason about its surroundings.

1973 In Scotland a robot called Freddy 2 that can assemble objects from a pile of parts is built. Victor Scheinman develops Puma (Programmable Universal Manipulation Arm), a programmable industrial robot arm.

1979   Hans Moravec builds the Stanford Cart, a robot that can find its own way across a room full of obstacles.

1989   Genghis, a walking robot, is built at Massachusetts Institute of Technology (MIT), USA.

1994   A robot called Dante 2 is developed for studying the gases inside volcanoes.

1996   The first virtual pop star, Kyoko Date, is created in Japan.
A robot fish called 'robo-tuna' is developed at MIT, USA.
In Japan, Honda develops a **prototype** robot, called P-2, which can walk and climb stairs.

1997   Gary Kasparov, the world chess champion, is beaten by IBM's Deep Blue computer.
The Sojourner robot, built by **NASA**, explores the surface of Mars.
Teams of robots compete for the first football RoboCup in Nagoya, Japan.

1998   MIT, USA, begin the development of Kismet, a robot that can mimic a human baby's emotions.

1999   Sony's robotic toy dog, Aibo, goes on sale.
The Cye robot is developed for doing jobs around the house.
A robot for taking blood from hospital patients is developed at Imperial College, London.
A robot worm for cleaning narrow pipes or blood vessels is developed in Germany.

2000   Over 700,000 robots are in use worldwide, more than half of them in Japan.
The virtual newsreader Ananova starts reading news stories on the **Internet**.
The Skyworker robot is developed at the Robotics Institute in Pittsburgh, Pennsylvania, USA, to help astronauts build and maintain large structures in space.
A **gastrobot**, developed at the University of South Florida, Tampa, USA, obtains energy by 'eating' sugar.
The brain of a lamprey fish is used to control a robot.
Honda unveils its latest walking robot, P-3.

2001   The Hyperion robot is developed at the Robotics Institute in Pittsburgh, Pennsylvania, USA, for exploring distant planets and moons.
A robot spy plane flies itself from the United States to Australia, a distance of 13,000 km (8078 miles).

2003   NASA plans to send two robots to the planet Mars.

Glossary

artificial neural network computer built in a way that mimics the structure of the human brain. See also **neural network**.

autonomous independent of any external control

computer simulations copies of things from the 'real world' that appear on computer screens

computing power ability of a computer to process information. Faster computers with bigger memories have the most computing power.

cookies short files of information created by a website. They are stored in an Internet user's computer so that the website can recognize repeat visitors.

cyber part of the word 'cybernetic'. Cyber is used with other words to indicate a connection with computers, particularly the Internet.

desktop computer that is small enough to sit on top of a desk and is not portable

distributed robotics building and using a robot system composed of a group of small robots that communicate with each other and co-operate to get a job done

expert systems machines that contain the acquired knowledge and experience of one or more experts in a particular subject, such as medicine

face recognition systems systems that scan human faces and compare them with faces stored in its memory in order to identify people

fuel cells devices used to produce electricity from a chemical reaction between hydrogen and oxygen

fuzzy logic type of decision-making program used by computers that can process imprecise or incomplete information, in a similar way to the human brain

gastrobot robot that powers itself by eating food and using microbes to digest it. The energy released from the food is converted into electricity.

hardware nuts, bolts and electronic circuits of a machine, such as a computer or robot

humanoid creature or robot that is similar to a human being

hyperlinks highlighted words, icons, buttons or images on a Web page that, when clicked on, takes the user directly to a new Web page

industrial robot robot used in industry, especially manufacturing, where it carries out jobs such as welding or painting that were previously done by people

infrared invisible energy waves used for communication

Internet global network of inter-linked computer networks

investments sums of money used to buy things in the hope that they become more valuable and will make a profit when they are sold

knowledge base stored information and rules used by an expert system to solve a problem or reach a decision

mainframe computers computers made from a large information processing unit connected to many keyboards and screens, called terminals

microbots small robots. There are no hard and fast rules for when a robot is small enough to be called a microbot. But most robots that are the size of a shoebox or smaller, down to about the size of a pea, are called microbots.

nanobots very small robots. Robots smaller than a few millimetres across are called nanobots. Some nanobots are so small that they can only be seen clearly through a microscope.

NASA The National Aeronautics and Space Administration. The US government agency that undertakes advanced flight research. All US manned space flights are managed by NASA.

natural language processing understanding speech and replying to it in the same way a person does

neural network information processing system made from information processing units called neurons connected together in a very complex way. The human brain is a neural network. A computer that copies this structure is called an artificial neural network.

program list of instructions that tell a computer what to do. Computer programs are also called software.

prosthetics replacement of real parts of the body with artificial parts. An artificial body part is called a prosthesis.

prototype first version of something that following copies are based on

real-time actual time when something happens. A live television broadcast is shown in real-time, when the event is actually happening, but a recorded video is not.

robot machine designed to carry out tasks in the place of a person or animal

search engines computer programs that look for Web pages containing words keyed in by the person using the search engine

sensors devices that detect or measure something

server computer that makes services available on a network

silicon substance found in sand that is used to make computer chips

simulated copied or imitated, especially using a computer. A computer simulation is created by programming a computer to show an object or copy a process.

software computer programs that make a computer or robot work

solar panels devices that change sunlight into electricity

sonar system for sensing what lies in front of a robot. It sends out bursts of high-pitched sound and picks up any reflections that bounce back from objects. Sonar stands for 'sound navigation and ranging'.

space probes unmanned spacecraft sent out to study the planets and their moons

space walks trips outside a spacecraft made by astronauts

surfer someone who clicks on hyperlinks to jump from page to page on the World Wide Web

three-dimensional having thickness in all three directions (length, breadth and depth), like objects in the real world

virtual reality version of reality created by a computer

virtual robots robots that are not machines, but exist only inside a computer's memory. They appear in a video screen, perhaps viewed using a virtual reality helmet. Wearing a data glove enables people to touch, pick up and move things in the virtual robot's world.

viruses unwanted computer programs that spread themselves from computer to computer through a network. Some viruses damage files in the computers they infect.

voice recognition system ability of a machine to understand spoken language

websites collections of related Web pages

wetware biological material used in robots

World Wide Web library on the Internet of millions of documents

Sources of information

Further reading

There are not many books written for school students on artificial intelligence and robots, but the following titles may be of interest:

Artificial Intelligence: Robotics and Machine Evolution, David Jeffries, Crabtree Publishing, 1999
Fast Forward: Robots, Mark Bergin, Hodder Wayland, 2001
How To Build A Robot, Clive Gifford, Oxford University Press, 2000
What's the Big Idea? Artificial Intelligence – Can Computers Think?, Jack Challoner, Hodder Children's Books, 1999
Focus: This monthly magazine deals with all aspects of popular science and technology, including robotics.

Websites

These websites are related to, or include stories about artificial intelligence, and may be of interest:

http://www.newscientist.com The website of the British science magazine *New Scientist*, with a searchable online library of articles on science and technology.

http://www.ri.cmu.edu The website of the Robotics Institute, part of the School of Computer Science, Carnegie Mellon University, USA.

http://www.aaai.org The website of the American Association for Artificial Intelligence.

http://www.humanoid.waseda.ac.jp The website of the Humanoid Robotics Institute, Waseda University, Japan.

http://www.ai.mit.edu The website of the Artificial Intelligence Laboratory, Massachusetts Institute of Technology, USA.

http://news.bbc.co.uk The BBC's online news archive includes stories and features about the latest developments in artificial intelligence and robots.

http://www.sciam.com *Scientific American* magazine's online archive includes articles about artificial intelligence and robots.

http://www.businessweek.com *Business Week* magazine's online archive includes articles about the business and commercial aspects of robotics.

Index

a-life (artificial life) 7,
  46–51
androids 20–1
artificial intelligence (AI) 6,
  7, 26, 28, 33, 44,
  51, 56
Asimov, Isaac 6, 8, 53
autonomous systems
  14–15
autonomous underwater
  vehicles (AUVs) 14

bank cash machines 29
biomimetics 15
brain, biological 22–3, 26,
  45, 46, 47, 49
brain, electronic 6, 9, 44,
  45, 46, 48

chess 28–9, 36
common sense 27
computer aided design
  (CAD) 43
computer simulations
  50, 51
cookies 45
creation of life 55
cyborgs 22
Cyc 27

decision-making 36
Deep Blue 28–9, 36
distributed robotics 34

electroactive polymer
  (EAP) 24, 25
electronic noses 39
emergency vehicle
  robots 10
emotions, artificial 32–3
energy supply 16
ethical issues 52–5
expert systems 36–43, 48
extra-terrestrial
  explorers 13

face recognition 26–7, 52
financial expert systems
  42–3
first commercial robot 8
fuzzy logic 25

Galaxy 31
games 26, 28–9, 29, 51
gastrobot 16
guards, robot 4, 5

hyperlinks 44

inference engine 36
intelligent robots 4–5, 7,
  9, 10, 13, 20, 26, 27,
  56

knowledge base 36

medical expert systems
  36, 38–41
medical robots 11–12
microbots 16, 34, 35
military applications 4, 5,
  48, 54–5
morphing robots 15
movement 15, 18
muscles 24, 25
musical composition 37
myoelectronics 19

nanobots 16, 17, 35
natural language
  processing 32
neural networks 46, 47,
  48, 49

personal robots 10
pros and cons of robots 9
prosthetics 19, 22

remote agents 15
reproduction 51
rights and responsibilities
  52, 55

robo-fish 4, 5, 15
Robo-monkey 18
robotics 6, 53

search engines 44
service robots 10
size, robot 16–17
software, intelligent 43
space probes 15
space robots 13
surgical robots 11

talking machines 29,
  31, 32
teamwork 34–5
transport robots 9
Turing Test 33

unmanned aerial vehicles
  (UAVs) 4, 5, 14
unmanned vehicles 9,
  14, 54

virtual robots 50–1
voice recognition 30–1,
  52, 56

wetware 23
World Wide Web 40,
  44–5

Titles in the *Science at the Edge* series include:

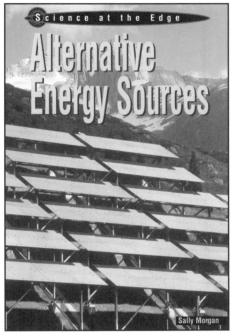

Hardback   0 431 14895 3

Hardback   0 431 14894 5

Hardback   0 431 14896 1

Hardback   0 431 14897 X

Find out about the other titles in this series on our website www.heinemann.co.uk/library